The Illustrated Story of President

DAVID O. McKAY

Great Leaders of The Church
of Jesus Christ of Latter-day Saints

The Illustrated Story of President David O. McKay
Great Leaders of The Church of Jesus Christ
of Latter-day Saints

Copyright © 1982 by
Eagle Systems International
P.O. Box 508
Provo, Utah 84603

ISBN: 0-938762-09-5
Library of Congress Catalog Card No.: 82-70265

Second Printing July 1983

First Edition

All rights reserved. No part of this publication may be reproduced or used in any manner or by any means—graphic, electronic, or mechanical, including photocopying, recording, taping, or information storage and retrieval systems—without written permission of the publisher.

Lithographed in U.S.A.
by
COMMUNITY PRESS, INC.

A Member of
The American Bookseller's Association
New York, New York

The Illustrated Story of President

DAVID O. McKAY

Great Leaders of The Church of Jesus Christ of Latter-day Saints

We thank the family of David O. McKay for their generous help and cooperation in this project.

AUTHOR
Joy N. Hulme

ILLUSTRATOR
B. Keith Christensen

DIRECTOR AND CORRELATOR
Lael J. Woodbury

ADVISORS AND EDITORS
Paul & Millie Cheesman
Mark Ray Davis
L. Norman Egan
Annette Hullinger
Beatrice W. Friel

PUBLISHER
Steven R. Shallenberger

A Biography Of DAVID O. McKAY

David Oman McKay was born to David and Jennette Evans McKay Sept. 8, 1873, in Huntsville, Utah. He was the third child and first son in a family of ten.

When he was seven years old, his two older sisters died in the same week. Shortly after this, his father went on a mission to Great Britain, leaving David to serve as the "man of the house."

In his youth he worked on the farm, delivered mail and newspapers, played the piano for the town band, and played second base on the ball team. As a young man, David hungered for a testimony and often prayed to the Lord for one. He felt that his prayers were not immediately answered, but when his testimony came to him as a missionary in Scotland, he realized that being obedient to God's will was more important than asking for a miraculous manifestation.

While laboring as a missionary, he saw a message carved over a doorway that he adopted as a motto: "Whate'er thou art, act well thy part."

He graduated from the University of Utah as president and valedictorian of his class and left that same year on his mission. When he returned, he taught as a faculty member at Weber Academy and married his college sweetheart, Emma Ray Riggs.

At the age of thirty-two he was ordained an apostle and spent nearly thirty years in the General Superintendency of the Sunday School as well as filling many other assignments as a General Authority. He was the first apostle in this dispensation to make a worldwide tour of the missions. After this year-long trip, he served as President of the European Mission, and then as a counselor to Presidents Heber J. Grant and George Albert Smith.

In 1951, at the age of seventy-eight, he became President of The Church of Jesus Christ of Latter-day Saints, which position he held until his death at ninety-six in 1970. He served longer as a General Authority than any other man, sixty-four years, and lived during the lifetimes of all the prophets in this dispensation except Joseph Smith.

His administration was a period of worldwide growth of the Church, during which he saw the long-existing prejudice against the Saints replaced with respect. In fact, he was personally responsible for much of this improved attitude. He made friends among members and nonmembers alike. He was a personal friend of several U.S. presidents and leading statesmen throughout the world. Dignitaries from many countries visited President McKay in Salt Lake City and greeted him in their own lands. One said of him, "If you were to fashion man in the image of God, there is the pattern."

President McKay was a gentle, kind, and loving man of stately and distinguished appearance. He was the tallest of the presidents at 6' 1" and weighed 195-200 lbs. He had flowing white hair, piercing hazel-brown eyes, and strong forceful features.

This humble farm boy was chosen by the Lord to lead his people, and through a life of selfless service to others, he grew to achieve greatness.

The air was as crisp as an autumn apple in Huntsville, Utah, the eighth day of September, 1873. A playful breeze was tickling the poplar leaves and inviting them to dance. Squirrels were scampering about stuffing their cheeks with nuts, but no one was noticing. Inside the McKay house something more important was happening. A new baby had arrived. We don't know her exact words, but the baby's mother may have whispered:

"Oh, David, a son. Isn't he wonderful?"

"Yes, indeed," the new father probably agreed. "The baby brother the girls have been coaxing for. Now they can play mother to a real doll."

"Let's call him David," Jennette urged. "I want him to be just like you."

"Won't two Davids be confusing?"

"Not if we give him a middle name too."

"How about Oman after Grandfather?"

Jennette may have tried the name on her tongue. "David Oman. Yes, I like that. We could call him David O."

"A boy needs a good solid name."

"You're right," Jennette laughed. Like any proud mother, she may have said: "You never know, he might grow up to be president."

"President of what?"

"I don't know. President of something important. President David O. McKay. How does that sound?"

David considered the proud tone in his wife's voice and studied the wise look on the face of his new son.

"Possible, my dear, highly possible," he may have replied.

David and Jennette were anxious to have their children do their best. They set good examples for their children. They taught them to work hard, to be honest, and to tell the truth. They learned to balance confidence with humility, kindness with firmness, thrift with generosity. They were inspired to pursue excellence in all things.

The little family continued to grow and before long David O. was like the cozy center of a sandwich with his older sisters, Margaret and Ellena, on one side and Thomas and Jennette on the other.

Then, just as fast and final as a slammed door, tragedy closed that happy chapter of life for the McKays. Margaret and Ellena were both dead. Within a week rheumatic fever had claimed one, pneumonia the other. At eleven and nine years of age, they lay side by side in the same grave.

"They always wanted to be together," Jennette choked, her heart heavy, her eyes dull.

"Why did they have to die?" David wanted to know. "WHY?"

"I can't tell you why," Mama said. "Only Heavenly Father knows that. We have to trust in his will."

"But I can't stand it!" he cried. "I will miss them too much."

"We will all miss them," she explained, "and someday we will understand. We know they are not gone forever. We'll be with them again."

She almost made it seem as if any day they might appear sitting on a cloud making hollyhock dolls for place cards at the dinner table. David O. could remember how Margaret would call to him, "Will you please bring some daisies for the hats?" Ellena preferred the jaunty look of larkspurs.

As the family gathered together in their grief, they found that "sorrow opens up the spaces of the heart and lets the glory out." They became even more precious to each other, more considerate, more trusting in the ways of the Lord.

For example, one night when David was very young, he lay thinking in his bed. He was lonely, even a bit frightened.

"I'm supposed to be the head of the family," he probably thought. "I want to be great and wonderful like Father. Instead, I am afraid of the dark! If only I could tiptoe into Mama's bedroom and hear her breathing, I would feel better. But what if she woke up? How could I tell her that I am afraid? She's counting on me to be brave."

He pulled the pillow tightly around his head, trying to hide from the darkness. Only God could help him now. Slowly he rolled out of bed onto his knees and poured out his fears to Heavenly Father. He talked for a long time. When he finished, the silence was deep. A quiet voice answered him.

"Don't be afraid," it said. "Nothing will hurt you."

A sweet peace filled his heart. He knew the Lord would protect him. He would never be afraid again. He jumped back into bed and fell asleep.

One day Father came into the house carrying the mail. His hands were shaking, his face was pale.

"David, what is it?" Mama asked.

"A letter from Box B," David's Father replied.

"Open it! Open it!" David O. shouted. He had heard of the famous Box B.

"I can't," Father said.

"Of course you can," Mama encouraged. "It's a great honor to get a letter from Box B."

"But it's impossible for me to go on a mission," Father insisted. "I can't leave you now. Not without the girls to help you and with the new baby coming. I need to get the addition built on the house. I'll just have to ask the Brethren to postpone the call to a more convenient time."

"Let me see that letter," Mama insisted.

Father handed it to her and she opened it and read it.

"To Scotland!" she shouted. "The place where you were born! Of course you will go. Don't worry about me. David O. and I will manage nicely. The Lord wants you to go on that mission now, not a year from now. He will take care of us."

THINK ABOUT IT:

1. How did David overcome his fear of the dark?
2. Why was it difficult for his father to go on a mission?
3. When a call comes from the Lord at an inconvenient time, what should you do about it?

When David McKay left on his mission in April of 1881, his last words to David O. were, "Take care of your mother." Young David was only seven, but until his father returned, he would be the man of the house. He was determined to do his best.

Sometime later Annie was born. This sweet little baby brought happiness and singing back into the McKay home. She was like a message sent from heaven.

That spring members of the priesthood quorums helped plant the grain, and the summer brought a good crop of hay. Grain prices were low at harvest time, so the yield was stored until spring, when it brought a good profit.

A hired man helped with the chores while Father was away. Mama was concerned about the cattle, especially the oxen, that they might not be getting enough to eat. One evening after the hired man had gone home, she took Thomas E. and David O. out to the barn, where the hay was stored. She and Thomas E. pulled hay from the stack and piled it in David's arms to carry to the animals. After five or six trips he could tell that those beasts would eat hay all night if they had the chance. He was getting tired of the job, so the next time he took an extra big load, dropped it quickly, and ran out.

"Hurry, Mama," he urged. "Let's get out of here before they eat that and want some more."

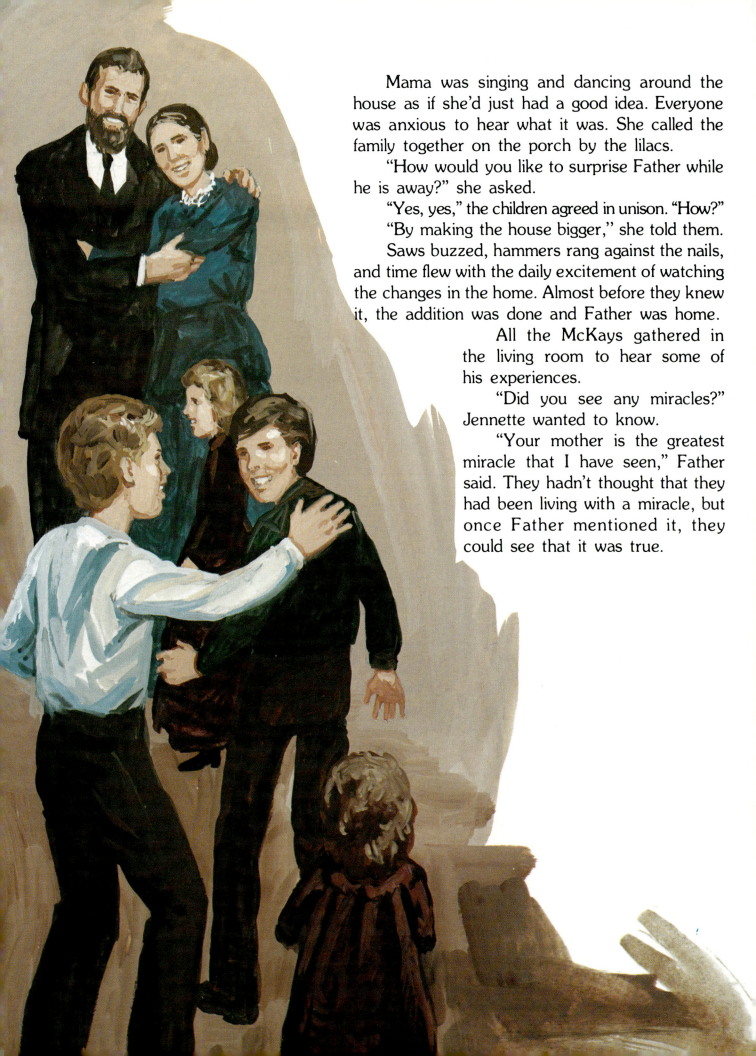

Mama was singing and dancing around the house as if she'd just had a good idea. Everyone was anxious to hear what it was. She called the family together on the porch by the lilacs.

"How would you like to surprise Father while he is away?" she asked.

"Yes, yes," the children agreed in unison. "How?"

"By making the house bigger," she told them.

Saws buzzed, hammers rang against the nails, and time flew with the daily excitement of watching the changes in the home. Almost before they knew it, the addition was done and Father was home.

All the McKays gathered in the living room to hear some of his experiences.

"Did you see any miracles?" Jennette wanted to know.

"Your mother is the greatest miracle that I have seen," Father said. They hadn't thought that they had been living with a miracle, but once Father mentioned it, they could see that it was true.

One summer David took a job carrying *The Ogden Standard,* a daily paper, to LaPlata, a booming mining town beyond Middlefork Canyon. This brought some extra money, but even better, it gave him the opportunity to make friends among the miners. He received a welcome fit for a king when he rode into town every day about noon with the latest news.

He had to leave home by seven o'clock in the morning and did not get back until nearly five in the afternoon. The long ride over the hills gave him a great deal of time to enjoy nature and to think about the choices he needed to make. He spent many hours thinking about a testimony. He knew this was the most precious thing a man could obtain in this life. He hungered for one. More than once he knelt by a serviceberry bush to pray.

David's patriarchal blessing contained promises that strengthened the feeling of destiny given him by his parents.

"The eye of the Lord is upon thee . . . ," it said. "The Lord has work for thee to do, in which thou shalt see much of the world, assist in gathering scattered Israel, and also labor in the ministry. It shall be thy lot to sit in council with the Brethren and preside among the people. . . ."

He did not understand all of this completely, but it was enough for him to know that the Lord had work for him to do. He did everything he could to prepare himself for this work. He was eager to serve. He was active in the presidencies of the deacons and teachers quorums, helping organize groups to clean the chapel and chop wood for the widows in the ward every week. When he was fifteen, he became secretary of the Sunday School, and four years later, a teacher.

What fun the young people had together! Horseback riding on the ranges, swimming in cold Spring Creek, baseball on the town square, acting in the dramatic series, debating, and glee club. David O. played the piano for the town's dance orchestra, which traveled to neighboring communities to liven up the young people.

During the summer they would pull timber down from the high mountains through the brush to the waiting wagon. A load was piled high and taken home to be stored in a large barn and used, as needed, for firewood or fenceposts.

When winter came they would bundle up in heavy coats and their warmest mittens, hitch a team of horses to the bobsled, and load the straw-filled wagon box with friends for a crispy-cold ride through the lanes of the valley, while sleigh bells jingled to the rhythm of the horses' pace.

One year David O. tamed a magpie and taught it to talk. Another time he left a window open in a saddle shed because it was the only entrance the birds had to their nest inside.

One autumn day in 1894 a strange procession wound its way over the ridge from Huntsville to Salt Lake City. The wagon was loaded with home-bottled fruit and vegetables, freshly ground flour, assorted boxes of pots and pans, books, and clothing. Four of the McKay children, David O., Thomas E., Jennette, and Annie, were on their way to the University of Utah. A trailer followed containing the cow that was to provide their dairy needs. They rented a house and settled down to go to school.

The second year they rented a cottage from Mrs. O. H. Riggs. David was soon attracted to her beautiful daughter, Emma Ray.

College days were filled to the brim with busyness: learning, athletics, music, friends, and romance. David played on the football team, was president of his class, and also was chosen to be valedictorian and address the graduating students.

As soon as he finished college, he planned to get a teaching job and earn money to help with family finances. Educating four children at the university was using up the McKay family resources. Four more at home were awaiting their turn to go. He succeeded. He was offered a teaching position in Salt Lake County.

Then came the letter that changed his life: a mission call to Scotland, land of his ancestors.

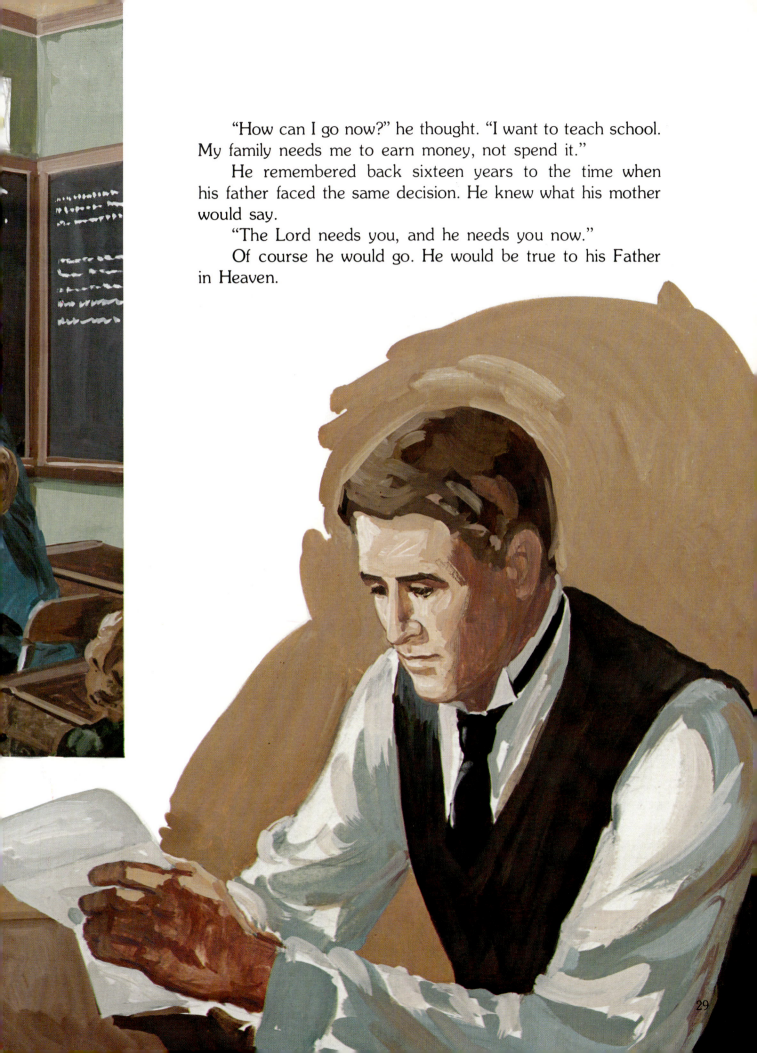

"How can I go now?" he thought. "I want to teach school. My family needs me to earn money, not spend it."

He remembered back sixteen years to the time when his father faced the same decision. He knew what his mother would say.

"The Lord needs you, and he needs you now."

Of course he would go. He would be true to his Father in Heaven.

David O. McKay had been in Scotland long enough to learn that converting people was not going to be easy. There was a great deal of prejudice against the Mormons. It seemed as if no one even wanted to speak to him, much less to hear about the gospel.

One day as he and his companion were walking into town, there was a partly-finished house with an unusual carving in stone over the door.

"Look at that," he said to Elder Johnston. "I wonder what it says."

"There's one way to find out," Elder Johnston replied. David walked up the gravel path to take a closer look.

"*Whate'er thou art*," he read, "*act well thy part.*"

The message burned in his heart.

"I am a missionary for Jesus Christ," he thought. "I will act my part well."

He put discouragement behind him, and with much fasting and praying, he plunged into the work.

THINK ABOUT IT:
1. What does it mean to act your part well?
2. What is *your* part?
3. How can you act it well?

Not long after that, at a conference priesthood meeting in the mission, the spiritual feeling was so great that one man present jumped to his feet and said, "Brethren, there are angels in this room."

Strong men were weeping, not from sorrow or fear, but for joy.

The presiding authority, President James L. McMurrin, arose and said, "Yes, there are angels in this room and one of them is the guardian angel of that man sitting there." He pointed to an elder who was weeping with happiness. He identified another of the angels present as well. Everyone in the room knew that what he said was true.

Later when he spoke to David, his words made an unforgettable impression.

"Let me say to you, Brother David, Satan hath desired to sift you as wheat, but God is mindful of you. *If you will keep the faith, you will sit in leading councils of the church.*"

Just like a focusing lens, David's future became clear to him. He knew he would spend most of the rest of his life in the service of the Lord. A miraculous, convincing change came over him. He felt encircled in the arms of his Heavenly Father's love. His youthful prayers on the hills of Huntsville were answered at last in this land far across the sea. Because of his searching prayers and hard work, his burning testimony of the divinity of the work had come.

As soon as he returned from the mission field, David O. began teaching at Weber Academy in Ogden, Utah. He and Emma Ray Riggs were married Jan. 2, 1901, the first couple sealed in the Salt Lake Temple in the twentieth century. After two years of teaching, he served as principal of the academy for several years.

In April of 1906 he was called, as his patriarchal blessing had promised, "to sit in council with the Brethren" as a member of the Quorum of the Twelve Apostles.

As a General Authority, he spent nearly thirty years in the General Superintendency of the Sunday School. The Lord needed his training and experience as a teacher and principal to strengthen this organization.

During this same time he had many other assignments as well.

In December of 1920 he received an unusual call to a year-long tour of all the missions of the Church. No other General Authority had ever done this.

He began his trip by dedicating the land of China to missionary work, then continued on to the South Sea Islands, toward Australia. . . .

In the little Maori village near Huntly, New Zealand, the Saints of the Puketapu Branch were preparing for a very special event. The first General Authority ever to visit their country was coming to the mission conference in April. Meeting tents and sleeping tents had to be provided. Great quantities of kumara (sweet potato), meat, and vegetables must be gathered to feed the expected crowd. Stuart Meha had been selected to interpret for the visitor so the local people could "fill their baskets" with every word and thought of this great man.

When David O. McKay stood before these faithful Saints, how he longed to speak to them in their native language! Since he could not, he prayed that through the Spirit they might receive an understanding of the things he would say.

Then a miracle happened. As the sermon proceeded: "It's alright, Brother Meha. You don't need to translate. We understand Brother McKay perfectly." The entire congregation had received the gift of interpretation of tongues.

After his first world tour of the missions, he became President of the European Mission. He later served as a counselor to Presidents Heber J. Grant and George Albert Smith.

In 1951, at the age of seventy-eight, he was called to "preside among the people" as President David O. McKay, Prophet, Seer, and Revelator of The Church of Jesus Christ of Latter-day Saints.

As President he continued to "see much of the world and assist in gathering scattered Israel." He traveled over two million miles, visiting the Saints, making friends with world leaders, promoting missionary work, and testifying of Jesus Christ.

He was greatly responsible for the change in attitude of the world toward Mormonism. During his leadership the walls of prejudice that he found on his mission crumbled, and the Church became highly regarded in all parts of the world.

Everywhere he went, he was loved by Church members and nonmembers alike. Each person was important to him as an individual. Time and time again he made this clear by acts of tender concern.

One of President McKay's outstanding characteristics was his prophet-like appearance. He was described as "tall, stately, and vigorous, with flowing white hair, piercing hazel-brown eyes, and a kindly smile. His strong character shone from his handsome face." It was said of him, "If you were to fashion man in the image of God, there is the pattern."

During the nineteen years of his presidency, the Church experienced astounding growth. The records say, "Nearly 4,000 new buildings were constructed, including eight temples; Church membership doubled; missionary work was expanded; the gospel was taken to far countries; and the Church was established worldwide. A full account of his leadership would fill many volumes."

When death came quietly on January 18, 1970, this great prophet had lived nearly a century (ninety-six years). He had served sixty-four years as a General Authority, longer than any other man. ("Thou shalt . . . labor in the ministry. . . .")

Through a life of selfless service, sacrifice, and acceptance of God's will, a humble farm boy had grown to greatness.

Ever since the day he had seen the carving over the unfinished doorway when he was a missionary in Scotland, David Oman McKay had remembered and lived its message:

Whate'er thou art, act well thy part.

TESTIMONY

When the Savior was about to leave His apostles, he gave them a great example—of service. You remember, he girt himself with a towel and washed his disciples' feet. Peter, feeling it was a menial work for a servant, said, "Dost thou wash my feet? Thou shalt not wash my feet." The Savior answered, "If I wash not thy feet, thou hast neither lot nor part with me." "Nay then," said the chief apostle, "not my feet only, but my hands and my head." "No, those were washed and clean already. What I doest now thou dost not fully comprehend." And then He washed his feet and the others. Returning the basin to the side of the door, ungirding himself of the towel, putting on his robe, he returned to his position with the twelve and said, "Ye call me Lord and Master, and so I am. What thou hast seen me do, do ye also to one another. He that is greatest among you, let him be least."

God bless you brothers and sisters. May the spirit of this occasion remain in our hearts. May it be felt throughout the outermost parts of this earth, wherever there is a branch in all the world, that the spirit might be a unifying power, an increasing of the testimony of the divinity of this work—that it may grow in its influence for good in the establishment of peace throughout the world. I bear you my testimony, at the head of this church is our Lord and Savior, Jesus Christ. I know the reality of His existence, of His willingness to guide and direct the servants who serve Him. I know He restored, with his Father, to the Prophet Joseph Smith, the gospel of Jesus Christ in its fullness. I know that these brethren whom you've sustained today are men of God. I love them, and don't you think anything else. God's will has been done. May we have increased power to be true to the responsibilities He and you have placed upon us, I pray in the name of Jesus Christ, Amen.